Katharina Kurek

Instant Messaging and Cross Site Scripting (XSS)

GRIN - Verlag für akademische Texte

Der GRIN Verlag mit Sitz in München hat sich seit der Gründung im Jahr 1998 auf die Veröffentlichung akademischer Texte spezialisiert.

Die Verlagswebseite www.grin.com ist für Studenten, Hochschullehrer und andere Akademiker die ideale Plattform, ihre Fachtexte, Studienarbeiten, Abschlussarbeiten oder Dissertationen einem breiten Publikum zu präsentieren.

Document Nr. V192840

Katharina Kurek

Instant Messaging and Cross Site Scripting (XSS)

GRIN Verlag

Bibliografische Information der Deutschen Nationalbibliothek: Die Deutsche Bibliothek verzeichnet diese Publikation in der Deutschen Nationalbibliografie; detaillierte bibliografische Daten sind im Internet über http://dnb.d-nb.de/ abrufbar.

1. Auflage 2011
Copyright © 2011 GRIN Verlag GmbH
http://www.grin.com
Druck und Bindung: Books on Demand GmbH, Norderstedt Germany
ISBN 978-3-656-18746-2

Instant Messaging and Cross-Site Scripting (XSS)

Katharina Kurek

Term Paper

at

Chair for Network and Data Security
Prof. Dr. Jörg Schwenk

advised through Mario Heiderich

22.02.2011

Horst-Görtz Institute   Ruhr-University of Bochum

Contents

List of Figures

Listings

1 Abstract

Cross-Site Scripting is a wide-spread kind of attack. It has been reported and exploited since the 1990s and became more and more important in the era of Web 2.0. Roughly 80 percent of all security vulnerabilities are Cross-Site Scripting [Syman2007]. But Cross-Site Scripting has always been a web application security hole so far and everyone focused on secure programming of web applications. In addition to this, there are many more possibilities of data exchange like instant messaging. Instant messaging clients were developed further and are now able to interpret HTML. This new potential of security holes is the emphasis of this work. The focus is on the question: Is it possible to execute JavaScript in file system context?

2 Introduction

Ever since the era of Web 2.0 we need to be concerned about security issues. At that time web application spread like wildfire and all companies wanted to be able to keep up to stay marketable. It was the age of the first online banking, online shopping and social network-applications and it was a growing sector where everybody wanted to have a share. Connected with the rapid tempo of programming web applications, security issues fell by wayside. Media reports about "hacker attacks" became more frequent. The necessity of counter-measures came up and as a consequence the Open Web Application Security Project (OWASP) originated [Owasp2010]. The OWASP TOP Ten Project was founded to classify the most important top ten security problems of web applications in 2004 (first release). The next release was published in 2007. Some of the most common attacks were named different and some of the attacks were new. The last release was published in April 2010. In second place one can find Cross-Side Scripting (figure 2.1).

Figure 2.1: OWASP Top Ten Project release 2010

Cross-Site Scripting, better known as XSS, occur whenever an application takes data originated from a user and sends it to a web browser without first validating or encoding that content. It has been reported and exploited since the 1990s and were roughly 80 percent of all security vulnerabilities documented by Symantec as of 2007 [Syman2007]. Considering that many web applications (like online banking- or e-commerce application) deal with money or user data, Cross-Site Scripting attacks can become a great danger.

Instant Messaging (IM) registered a similar growth. First appearing on a multi-user operating systems like CTSS and Multics in the mid-1960s, modern and GUI-based messaging began to take off in the mid 1990s with PowWow, ICQ and AOL message [Insta2001]. Today current IM clients can even be installed on mobile devices like smartphones and tablets and are a widespread form of communication. But what do Instant Messaging and Cross-Site Scripting have in common? This work deals with the possibility of executing XSS not only in context of web applications, but also after being delivered by an instant messaging client.

3 Overview

3.1 Cross-Site Scripting (XSS)

Cross-Site Scripting, better known as XSS, is the most far spread web application security issue. It is in fact a subset of HTML injection and the most prevalent and pernicious vulnerability of web applications. XSS enables malicious attackers to inject client-site script into web pages viewed by other users (Stored XSS) or viewed by the victim himself once (Reflected XSS). An exploited Cross-Site Scripting vulnerability can be used for executing script in the victims's browser, which can hijack user sessions, deface web sites, insert hostile content, conduct phishing attacks, and take over the user's browser using scripting malware.

3.1.1 Reflected XSS

Reflected (or non-persistent) XSS is the easiest to exploit - a page will reflect user supplied data directly back to the user. A classic example of a potential vector is a site search engine: if one searches for a string, the search string will typically be redisplayed verbatim on the result page to indicate what was searched for (figure 3.1). Such a hole shows up when the data provided by a web client, most commonly in HTTP query parameters or in HTML form submissions, is used immediately by server-side scripts to generate a page of results for that user, without properly sanitizing the request. If the victim owns extended rights (administrators, owner of bank accounts), it is even possible for the attacker to attain possession of all of the victim's privileges [OwXss2010].

3.1.2 Stored XSS

The stored (or persistent) XSS vulnerability is extremely dangerous in systems such as CMS, blogs, or forums, where a large number of users will see input from other individuals. Stored XSS takes hostile data, stores it in a file, a database, or other back-end systems and then at a later stage, displays the unfiltered data to the user. This kind of XSS exploit is such devastating, because an attacker's malicious script is rendered automatically, without the need to individual target victims or lure them to a third-party website. For example, malicious comment placed in a comment field of a social network website (figure 3.1) would be executed every time a user opens the malicious user profile containing the comment of the attacker [OwXss2010].

3.1.3 DOM injection

With DOM based XSS attacks, the site's JavaScript code and variables are manipulated rather than HTML elements. This kind of attack will be executed on the victim's client and was first

Figure 3.1: Reflected XSS using a search engine

Figure 3.2: Stored XSS using a comment field

described by Admin Klein in his paper "Dom Based Cross Site Scripting or XSS of the Third Kind" [Klein2005]. By using DOM elements the attacker is able to address and manipulate them. Steeling a cookie with DOM based XSS is typical example of using this form of XSS (listing 3.1) [OwXss2010].

Listing 3.1: DOM-based attack stealing victim's cookie

```
http ://www. example .com/ index . html ?name=<script>document. location=
'http :// attackerhost . example / cgi−bin / cookiesteal . cgi ?'
+document . cookie</ script>
```

2

3.2 Instant Messaging and Cross-Site Scripting (XSS)

Instant messaging (IM) clients are a dime a dozen. Once built for simple text-based communication with two ore more people, it is now capable of utilizing different types of communication like sending birthday cards, flash animated messages and files. But what has instant messaging to do with Cross-Site Scripting? As mentioned at the beginning of this work, XSS used to be the most relevant hacking technique in connection with web applications, but why do we now connect instant messaging and XSS? Well, with the years, instant messaging was getting more and more complex. Its was not only possible to send simple text, but also to affect its look by using HTML (figure 3.3).

Figure 3.3: HTML interpreted text which was sent with an Instant Messaging Client

The usage of HTML implies the possibility of vulnerabilities, if security has not been threatened as a main aspect. ICQ is the most popular IM-client and will be the main tested IM client in this work.

3.2.1 ICQ

ICQ is an instant messaging computer program, which was first developed and popularized by the israeli company Mirabilis. First Mirabilis was established in 1996 by five Israelis: Yair Goldfinger, Sefi Vigiser, Amnon Amir, Arik Vardi, and Arik's father Yossi Vardi [ICQC2011]. They recognized that many people were online accessing the internet through a non-UNIX operating system, and that there was no software that enabled an immediate connection between them. The missing part was the technology for locating and connecting the users of the Windows operating system. The first version of the program was released in November 1996 and ICQ became the first internet-wide instant messaging service, later patenting the technology [ICQB2007]. Later it was bought by America Online [ICQB2007], and since April 2010 owned by Mail.ru Group [ICQC2011].The name "ICQ" is an adaptation of the Morse code callout "CQ", which means "calling any station". According to Time Warner [Warne2001], ICQ has over 100 million accounts registered. ICQ's features are

- sending text messages

- offline support

- multi-user chats

- free daily-limited SMS sending

- resumable file transfers

- greeting cards

- multiplayer games

- searchable user directory

and many more.

ICQ as sending-client First naive sending of a test vector with ICQ revealed some problems. It seemed that sending HTML-formated text with ICQ has not been interpreted. The chosen test vector was

```
<i>italic</i>
```

which should appear on the recipient's side as
italic

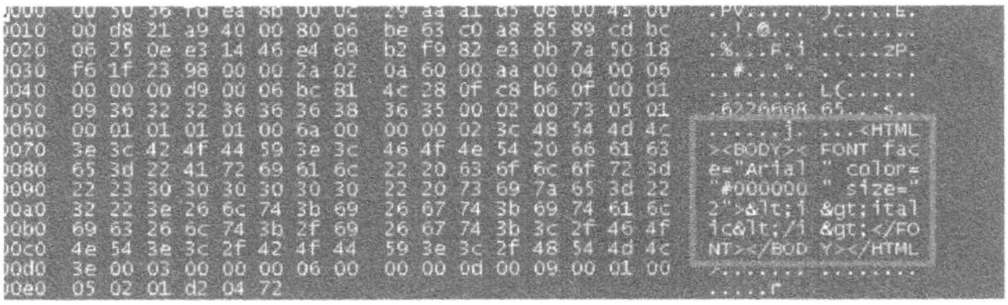

Figure 3.4: ICQ-sent package viewed in Wireshark

Figure 3.4 shows the content of a package sent with ICQ v7.2 build: 3525. In view is first a classic HTML-structure with tags like `<html>` and `<body>`. Within the body-tag one can see the sent message text which seems to have been encoded to

`&lt;i&gt;italic&lt;/i/i&gt;`

The conclusion after watching the package with a tool named "Wireshark" [Wire2011](client for scanning network traffic, see chapter 4.1) is to choose another sending client. If messages are changed before sending, one can hardly verify the success of a test vector.

4

3.2.2 Miranda IM

Miranda IM is an open source multi protocol instant messaging application. It is free software distributed under GNU General Public License. It provides a basic client framework and also an advanced plugin architecture. The implementation of optional plugins allows the usage of various IM protocols and additional features and some of them come bundled with Miranda IM by default. There are over 500 available additional plugins, which are available on the official add-ons site of Miranda IM [Miran2011]. Unused protocols can be removed.

Miranda IM as sending-client   The advantage of using Miranda IM as sending client became clear immediately after sending the same test-vector as used on testing ICQ in advance; there was so modification of the test vector with the simple italic text. But after sending messages containing tags like `<script>`, `<img scr=>` or the keyword `javascript` Miranda IM answered with an error. An analysis of the network traffic showed; no package was sent. So Miranda IM blocks malicious keywords right before sending. As a consequence Miranda IM is not qualified to constitute the sending client in the test scenario of this work.

3.2.3 Pidgin

Pidgin is a multi-platform instant messaging client, based on a library named libpurple [Pidgi2011]. Libpurple has support for many commonly used instant messaging protocols allowing the user to log into various different services from one application. Pidgin provides a graphical front-end for libpurple and supports multiple operating systems. Pidgin and libpurple are free software, released under the terms of the GNU General Public Licence [Pidgi2011].

Pidgin as sending-client   After sending the same test-vector it turned out, that pidgin showed considerable similarities with the behavior of ICQ. Packages were altered before sending, which could be ascertained beyond doubt after analyzing sent packages with Wireshark.

3.2.4 Climm

Climm is the only text-based instant messaging client of all tested clients. It is very portable and was designed for Linux,Windows just as BSD, HPUX, AmigaOS and with some restrictions for BeOs. Originally written by Matthew D. Smith, a great part of Climm has been rewritten by Ruediger Kuhlmann, in particular the support for the new version 8 of the OSCAR protocol that became necessary, the internationalization, the file transfer and some restructuring of the code [Clim2011]. It is very simple and sends raw unmodified text without any filtering-mechanism. Any tests with Climm confirmed its adequacy for being the sending client.

Some of Climm's features are:

- login: with both the old v6 and the new v8 protocol

- register new UINs and setup configuration with an easy to use setup wizard

- changing password

5

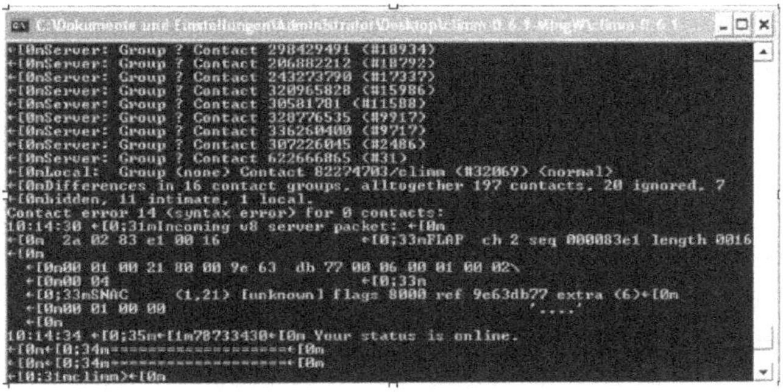

Figure 3.5: Climm Instant Messaging client

- reconnects when kicked by server

- complete contact list with several ways for a concise display of online/offline users

- set status arbitrarily

- send and receive messages and URLs

- send acknowledged messages to clients who understand them

- send UTF-8 encoded messages to clients who understand them

and many more [Clim2011].

4 Testing

4.1 Preparations

4.1.1 Platform adaptations

An important basis is the testing environment. To achieve informative results, it is essential to consider all marginal conditions beforehand. First, it is important not to affect the owners operating system with any testing activities. The solution in this matter is to use virtualization technologies like Virtual Box or Vmware. The advantage is that no system will be influenced by testing rather the sending machine nor the recipient. Furthermore it is important to ascertain a preferably genuine handling of the received data by the recipient's operating system. In this case it would be possible to find a conclusive result.

Chosen Platform for testing:

- **Operating System (sender and recipient:**Windows XP (SP3,August 2009), IE6.0.2900.5512,Opera 11.01 (for Win32) (virtualized by VMware).

- **IM Client as sender:** Climm 0.6.1 for Windows

- **IM Client as recipient:** ICQ 7.2 build: 3525

- **Network analysing tool:** Wireshark 1.4.3

- **Other tools:**Freeware Hex Editor XVI32 v2.51, Life (web-based) HTML Editor, Process Monitor 2.94

4.1.2 Analysing activities

Before starting the test, it might be interesting to find out which activities are run by ICQ while executed. Microsoft offers a tool names "Process Monitor" as freeware with which one can track all activities running in background. Process Monitor acts like an extended task manager and it is possible to filter each process and view its activities on the disc [Monit2011].The GUI of Process Monitor is easy to use, one has to possibility to search for a certain process to view its activities. In Figure 4.1 one can see all activities of the process ICQ.exe sorted chronologically .Figure 4.2 shows the first action ICQ.exe performs in the windows registry. Before connecting to the ICQ-server, ICQ.exe checks some privacy policies and trusted domain-settings.   Afterwards ICQ.exe accesses the Owners.qdb, which contains a hash value of the stored user-password of ICQ (if it is stored on hard disc). Thereupon ICQ.exe accesses the DLL-file MBContainer.dll which is an ICQ-file and will be threatened as a black box in this work.

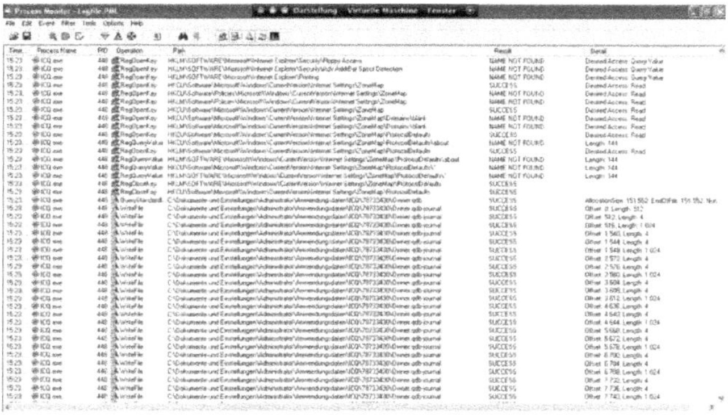

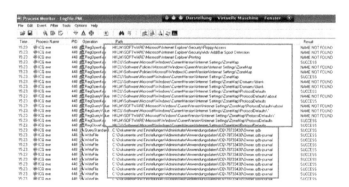

Figure 4.1: Process Monitor for analysing activities

Figure 4.2: Security settings and user-password

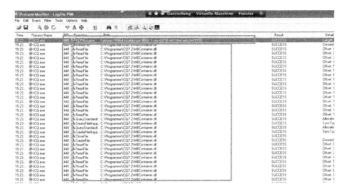

Figure 4.3: ICQ-file MBContainer.dll

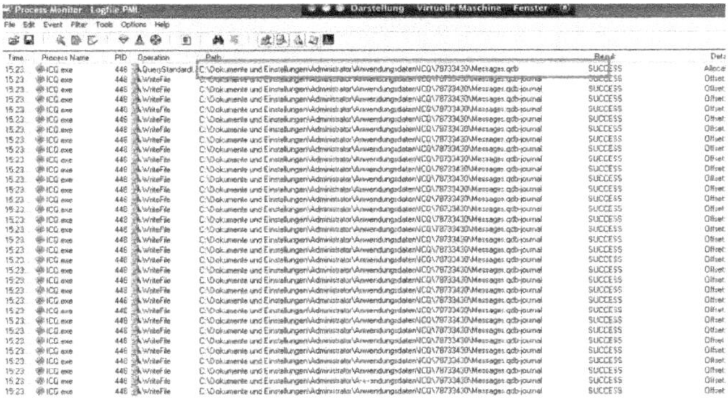

Figure 4.4: Messages temporary stored/cached in Messages.qdb

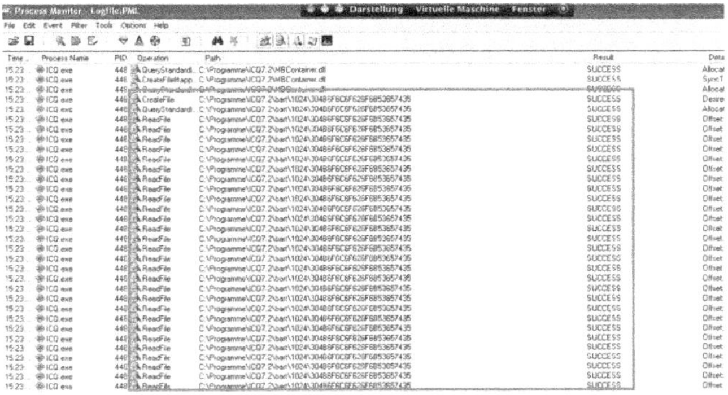

Figure 4.5: Animated smiley

Finally (figure 4.3), after a message was sent to this ICQ-client, Process Monitor shows a registered activity accessing the file Messages.qdb. A look in Messages.qdb (with the Hex Editor) shows, that this message seems to be stored/cached in this file. This is an important conclusion relating to JavaScript's capabilities. JavaScript itself can not access any resources of the user's file system, if it is executed in browser-context. Executed on the user's hard disc JavaScript execution implies more possibilities,namely code-execution in file system-context with user rights. One could get access to all files on the victim's hard disc.

Figure 4.5 shows the process which accesses the file referencing smileys and animated gifs.

Finally ICQ.exe creates a time stamp using quards.dll and executes the incoming.mp3 after loading the MP3-extension to announce the new incoming massage. With this knowledge we will start our series of test. The aim will be to execute JavaScript-code in file-system context. Afterwards ICQ.exe accesses the Owners.qdb, which contains a hash value of the stored user-password of ICQ (if it is stored on hard disc).

4.2 Message Box

ICQ's most obvious input option is its message box (Figure 4.6). The usage of the message box is the most common kind of sending messages. User use this input type to communicate with simple text, but also to send URLs and smilies. The aim will be to send some JavaScript code oder HTML code which - once delivered - will be executed on victim's machine. The following steps contain sending JavaScript "naive" (by sending test vectors of a XSS Cheat Sheet) and aimed sending by sending all possible HTML tag-combinations.

10

4.2.1 XSS Cheat Sheet

First of all we will start a kind of "naive testing" by sending an up to date XSS Cheat Sheet ([Heide2011] , [Hacke2011]). The aim is to receive an impression of how ICQ generally reacts to known malicious test vectors. [Hacke2011] is not up to date anymore, but its good enough for testing ICQ's behavior at first. Testing with the XSS Cheat Sheet crystallizes out a clear manner; no malicious testing vector of both XSS Cheat Sheets was successful. None of the malicious messages was executed and none of them caused any damage on victim's system. But while sending each test vector, one could spot different behavior on some of the sent vectors.

Figure 4.6: Message box of ICQ 7.2

Known "malicious" tags: It turned out, that sending certain HTML-tags cause a kind of blocking on recipient's side. While malicious messages sent with Climm were sent without being filtered , they were never delivered (both verified by Wirekshark). It seems as there is a filtering-system on server side, which prevents the recipient from even getting such a malicious package. This reaction occurred after sending vectors containing tags like `<script>`, `<img scr=>` and the keyword `<...javascript..>`.

Hiding "bad" tags in "good" tags: Testing with the XSS Cheat Sheet showed that there is no possibility to "hide" blocked tags in not-blocked tags like in listings 4.1 and 4.2.

Listing 4.1: Hiding "bad" tags in "good" tags

```
<comment><img src="</comment><img␣src=x␣onerror=alert(1))//">
```

or

Listing 4.2: Hiding "good" tags in "bad" tags

```
<style><img src="</style><img_src=x_onerror=alert(1)//">
```

While tags like `<comment></comment>` didn't cause any difficulties to pass the filter and were delivered, adding tags like `<script>` enclosed by such a comment tag was blocked immediately.

Using character encoding: Some of the XSS Cheat Sheet vectors use data encoding like base64. The aim is to alienate the known blocked keywords to bypass the filter. None of the encoded vector was successful and was blocked as same as the not-encoded vector.

The treatment of links: All tags until now appear to be checked for malicious content. It is not possible to hide keywords like `<script>` in tags not listed on the alleged blacklist. Links however, seem not to be affected by this handling. Its even possible to insert malicious content into a link-tag like in listing 4.3

Listing 4.3: Link containing a data URI

```
<a href="data:text/html,%3cscript>alert('hello')%3c/script>">click</script>
```

The content contains a data URI scheme, which works in Safari 5.0.3 (6533.19.4) and Opera 11.01 (for Wind32).After sending, the posted link was displayed as a URL (Figure 4.7), which appears harmless for the victim. On click the alert was executed (Figure 4.8), which demonstrated the possibility of creating phishing-attacks.

Figure 4.7: Link delivered and displayed

After changing the URL scheme into a data URI, one could try another attack using a different scheme as in listing 4.4.

Listing 4.4: Known attack to access victim's hard disc

```
<a href="file://127.0.0.1/c$/">click</a>
```

12

Figure 4.8: Link-content being executed

Listing 4.4 shows a known attack [Secli2009] working in the Internet Explorer. Once executed it enables the attacker to access the file system out of the internet browser in this example drive C:Sent with Climm, this vector was not delivered. It seems as if again there was a blacklisting. Trying to send all existing URL schemes undergirded the assumption of a blacklisting, because most of the sent URL schemes were delivered.

4.2.2 HTML Tags

Testing with the XSS Cheat Sheet is not enough and does not involve all existing HTML-tags. To find a conclusive result it is necessary to include the entire range of possible tags and combinations with attributes and events. A combination of all tags with all attributes and all events at once would overload the output of the php-script, which was created to combine all this items with each other automatically. So the first step should be to create a test vector which includes all existing HTML-tags without any attributes and events (listing 4.5). Msg 622666865 is the syntax for Climm to send a message to a certain UIN.

Listing 4.5: All HTML tags as test vector

```
msg  622666865  <blink>blink</blink>
msg  622666865  <marquee>marquee</marquee>
msg  622666865  <embed>embed</embed>
msg  622666865  <a>a</a>
. . .
```

After all tags were sent with Climm, none was blocked and each of the tag was interpreted by ICQ. As we know now, that none of all possible HTML-tags has been blocked, we can choose one of them to combine it with all existing attributes (listing 4.6).

Listing 4.6: Sending all attributes

```
msg  622666865  <body abbr="abcdef()">abbr</body>
msg  622666865  <body accept-charset="abcdef()">accept-charset</body>
msg  622666865  <body accesskey="abcdef()">accesskey</body>
msg  622666865  <body action="abcdef()">action</body>
```

13

. . .

All combined attributes were delivered, none was blocked. The urgent question that arises here is: is there any filter-mechanism that blocks anything but the "known malicious tags"? The last step now is to pick one of these tags and combine it with all known events that JavaScript implements (listing 4.7).

Listing 4.7: Sending all events

```
msg  622666865  <body  onabort="abcdef()">onabort</body>
msg  622666865  <body  onactivate="abcdef()">onactivate</body>
msg  622666865  <body  onafterprint="abcdef()">onafterprint</body>
msg  622666865  <body  onactivate="abcdef()">onactivate</body>
```
. . .

At last some of the malicious vectors were not delivered and apparently blocked. An analysis of the network-traffic with Wireshark assured this assumption. All of the blocked events seem to be part of a blacklist. The fact that up to 20 percent of the vectors were blocked, implies the usage of a blacklist. Most of the not-blocked events are new events supported not earlier than Opera 11, IE 8 and Firefox 3. The usage of a blacklist and the fact, that not many of the sent vectors were blocked by ICQ (maybe on server-side) offers new possibilities of testing. One could create a vector, which needs no user interaction and was not marked as blocked like in listing 4.8.

Listing 4.8: Sending an alert

```
msg  622666865  <body  onactivate=alert('1')>onactivate</body>
```

Figure 4.9 shows the reaction on recipient's side: it is obviously no problem to bypass the filter by using this test vector, but no execution of the alert takes place.

Figure 4.9: No blocking, no execution

14

4.2.3 CSS Expressions

Another possibility to execute JavaScript-code without using the keyword-tag `<script>` is to use CSS Expressions. CSS Expressions are a property of the Internet Explorer and allow the web-programmer to set a CSS property not to a constant, but to the result of a JavaScript expression [Micro2009] and are supported for web pages displayed in IE5 mode or IE7 mode.

Listing 4.9 shows an example of using CSS Expressions.

Listing 4.9: CSS Example

```
td.locked_left, th.locked_left {
    background-color: #88ff88;
    font-weight: bold;
    left:
    expression(document.getElementById('table_container').scrollLeft);
    border-left: 1px solid #ffffff;
    position: relative;
    z-index: 1
}
```

Listing 4.9 is an extract from a CSS-code. One can see, how expressions are used in this context. Instead of a constant, one is able to define JavaScript-code. What does this mean for creating test vectors? Well, one could try to create a test vector containing JavaScript code without announcing it with the signal-word `javascript` or using script-tags. A malicious test vector could be created like shown in listing /refexpressions.

Listing 4.10: Test vector using expressions

```
msg 622666865 <body onabort="expression()">onabort</body>
```

In chapter 4.2.2 we tried to deliver vectors like shown in listing 4.11.

Listing 4.11: Used test vectors

```
msg 622666865 <body onabort="abcdef()">onabort</body>
```

That makes sense after learning about CSS Expressions, which have actually a similar structure. If a function like `abcdef()` can be delivered, what about the function `expression()`? After sending a malicious message to the test-recipient nothing was delivered immediately. A look with Wireshark into the captured network-traffic showed, that nothing was delivered just as after sending messages containing other keywords like `<script>` and `<img scr=>`. Apparently "expression()" is also a part of the blacklist. But what about using data encoding in this case? Listing 4.12 shows how one could use data encoding.

Listing 4.12: Using data encoding- expressions containing script code

```
<body style="background-color:expression(write(1))">onabort</body>
<body style="background-color:ex\pression(write(1))">onabort</body>
<body style="background-color:&#x65x\pression(write(1))">onabort</body>
<body style="background-color:ex\pr\65ssion(write(1))">onabort</body>
<body style="background-color:ex\pr&#x5c;65_ssion(write(1))">onabort</body>
<body style="background-color:&#x65x\Pre&#83&#83iOn(write(1))">onabort</body>
```

15

All test vectors were validated with the HTML life editor and worked [Life2011]. However, sending this vectors was not successful and messages were blocked further on.

URLs, Birthday e-cards and chat   Of cause, there also are other different input types ICQ offers to use. Testing all the other input types like URLs, Birthday e-cards and chat resulted in the same conclusion as testing the message box. It seems like if there was an main engine for all text-input. Sending a birthday e-cards is only possible with the usage of the ICQ.com backend which seems to use input-validation.

4.3 Files

ICQ offers the possibility to send files between two clients. One is able to choose pictures just as text-files and even executable applications. Right before receiving a file, the user receives an pop-up message, which tells him/her, that opening files without being sure about the content could be compromising for the user's operating system. But for all that it could be necessary to check files before delivering them. There are two possibilities to insert malicious content into a file, before delivering it to the victim:

- the name of a file
- the content of a file

4.3.1 Maliciously Formed Names

The first step will be to send a file with a maliciously formed name, which is actually a JavaScript-code executing an alert-box.

```
<img src=x onerror=alert(1)>.jpg
```

Sending this file with a Windows operating system might cause problems because of the name of the file containing special characters. One can use a Unix-based operating system to send this malicious file without any problems. While trying to send the prepared file, the sending IM-client displays an error before even sending anything; it claims that the connection was canceled by the recipient. A look at the recipient's side turns out, that the recipient also got an error posted by ICQ, which tells that "no transfer is possible". This clearly implies, that the connection was refused by ICQ itself and no transfer of a malicious-named file is possible.

4.3.2 Malicious Content

PNG files   There is another possibility to send a prepared file with malicious content. Instead of changing its name, one can change its content. Pictures are proper for being sent to a victim, because they appear to be harmless compared to applications (*.EXE). So one could just prepare a PNG file with JavaScript code within and send it to the victim. This actually does not work, because ICQ throws error-messages which tell that "this picture seems not valid". Obviously,

ICQ checks files for being valid in advance. But there is a possibility to make files appear valid. One could create a valid PNG file with a picture editor like gimp. Let aside the content, mentionable is the comment one can insert right before saving the picture file. Gimp asks the user to insert a comment which could actually be script code for this test scenario (figure **??**)

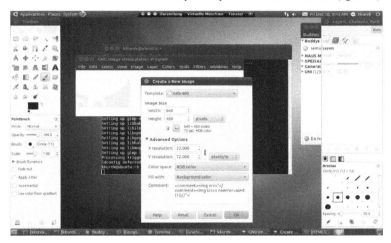

Figure 4.10: Picture file with JavaScript code as comment

After sending one can verify, that the file has been transfered properly without any errors. No execution occurs, but in some context this kind of attack might be successful.

SVG   Scalable Vector Graphics (SVG) is a family of specifications of an XML-based file format for describing two-dimensional vector graphics, both static and dynamic. SVG images and their behaviors are defined in XML text files. This means that they can be searched, indexed, scripted and, if required, compressed [SVG2011]. They also can be edited with a simple text-editor.

Listing 4.13: Simple SVG-file

```
<?xml version="1.0" standalone="no"?>
<!DOCTYPE svg PUBLIC "-//W3C//DTD_SVG_1.1//EN"
        "http://www.w3.org/Graphics/SVG/1.1/DTD/svg11.dtd">

<svg version="1.1" baseProfile="full"
        xmlns="http://www.w3.org/2000/svg">
    <polygon id="triangle" points="0,0_0,50_50,0"
```

17

```
                    fill="#009900"  stroke="#004400"/>
</svg>
```

Listing 4.13 shows a simple SVG-file which draws a green triangle in the left side of the screen. To create a malicious SVG-file that pops up an alert-box on victim's screen, one can insert JavaScript-code (Listing 4.14)

Listing 4.14: Malicious SVG-file

```
<?xml version="1.0" standalone="no"?>
<!DOCTYPE svg PUBLIC "-//W3C//DTD␣SVG␣1.1//EN"
        "http://www.w3.org/Graphics/SVG/1.1/DTD/svg11.dtd">
<svg version="1.1" baseProfile="full" xmlns="http://www.w3.org/2000/svg">
    <polygon id="triangle" points="0,0␣0,50␣50,0"
                    fill="#009900" stroke="#004400"/>
    <script type="text/javascript">
       alert('1');
    </script>
</svg>
```

Listing 4.14 shows a script-tag containing a code-snippet which -once delivered and executed-will pop up an alert-box on user's machine. Sending this file is no problem (even with ICQ 7.2 as sender). Again, ICQ seems only to check if the SVG-file is valid and does not check the malicious content. After transfer, the SVG-file can be found in the default folder for downloads on victim's hard disc.

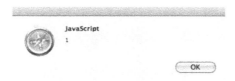

Figure 4.11: SVG-file opened with Safari 5.0.3 (6533.19.4)

Figure 4.11 demonstrated the execution of the SVG-file which works good with Safari 5.0.3 (6533.19.4) and Opera 11.01 (for Win32). Evidently, the JavaScript-code included in the SVG-file was executed on user's machine. In chapter 4.2.2 we learned about JavaScript-code being executed in file-system context. The next step might be to prove this statement. We thusly change to JavaScript-code within the SVG file (Listing 4.15):

Listing 4.15: Malicious SVG-file with file-access

```
<?xml version="1.0" standalone="no"?>
<!DOCTYPE svg PUBLIC "-
␣␣␣//W3C//DTD␣SVG␣1.1//EN"
```

18

```
                   "http://www.w3.org/Graphics/SVG/1.1/DTD/svg11.dtd">

<svg version="1.1" baseProfile="full" xmlns="http://www.w3.org/2000/svg">
    <polygon id="triangle" points="0,0 0,50 50,0"
                    fill="#009900" stroke="#004400"/>

        <script type="text/javascript">
          window.open("*.exe", "Window2", "width=300,height=200,scrollbars=yes");
        </script>
</svg>
```

Listing 4.15 now contains a JavaScript-code snippet, which simply opens a new window. This window shows all content of the folder in which this code has been executed. The result after the successful transfer can be regarded in Figure 4.12.

Figure 4.12: SVG-file opened with Opera 11 showing folder content filtered by *.exe

It is seemingly possible to execute JavaScript-code in file-system context. If we get access to the file system, we can go one step further and cause some damage.

- DOM-based attacks: it is possible to load a known page and steal user's cookie thereafter.

- Attacks using XMLHttpRequest: with some AJAX-techniques one could read all content of the folder where the SVG-file is executed and send it to a any URL on the web.

Executing JavaScript code by just opening a SVG file is dangerous and should not be allowed by internet browsers. ICQ should not allow the transfer of SVG files.

19

5 Conclusion

ICQ is a very wide-spread tool which makes many people interconnected. It is much used and this is why programmers should agitate about security issues. Dealing with HTML/JavaScript in non-browser context could be a danger and should be treated as a main aspect. There was a great hype concerning web application security and the related implementation of the web applications. But did this alertness also include all applications which deal with HTML/JavaScript? Previous testing gave us an impression of the constitution of ICQ's security implementation. The apparent usage of a blacklist does not fulfill the best practices proposal of OWASP [Owasp2009] which might be exploited eventually by using a zero day exploit not being on the blacklist. Filtering of files is missing completely. One is able to send any content to the victim, although it seems not to be a dangerous file format. SVG and picture in general are a great danger. Not only by the implementation of the browser, which actually allows to implement script code in a picture, but also by ICQ which allows sending a SVG file without being validated. With these "security holes" ICQ could be alienated and used like an "entrance gate" to user's file system. Security issues have often been neglected in the past. The consequences appeared in the media and let us learn to deals with security issues as an important main aspect. But not only web applications should be affected by this new upcoming attention. One should think one step ahead and also treat the implementation of other application like instant messaging clients with care.

Bibliography

[Klein2005] Amit Klein: DOM Based Cross Site Scripting or XSS of the Third Kind. http://www.webappsec.org/projects/articles/071105.shtml, ACM Press, April 2005.

[Warne2001] Time Warner Newsroom: ICQ Celebrated 100 Million Registred Users. http://www.timewarner.com/corp/newsroom/pr/0,20812,668719,00.html, Time Warner Press, May 2001.

[Heide2011] Mario Heiderich:HTML5 Security Cheatsheet. http://heideri.ch/jso/, January 2011.

[Hacke2011] Ha.chers.org: XSS (Cross Site Scripting) Cheat Sheet Esp: for filter evasion. http://ha.ckers.org/xss.html, January 2011.

[Micro2009] Microsoft.com: About Dynamic Properties. http://msdn.microsoft.com/en-us/library/ms537634(v=vs.85).aspx, Microsoft.com, September 2009.

[Xssed2008] Xssed.com: Cross Site Scripting - Attack and Defense Guide. http://www.xssed.com, XSSED.com, February 2008.

[Secli2009] Seclist.org: Internet Explorer Security Zone restrictions bypass. http://seclists.org/fulldisclosure/2009/Jun/91, Seclist.org, June 2009.

[Owasp2010] Owasp.org: OWASP Top 10 for 2010.http://www.owasp.org, OWASP Top Ten Project, April 2010.

[Syman2007] Symantec.org :Symantec Internet Security Threat Report. http://eval.symantec.com/, December 2007.

[Insta2001] Multicians.org: The History of Electronic Mail .http://www.multicians.org/thvv/mail-history.html , Multicians.org, February 2001.

[OwXss2010] Owasp.org: Cross-site Scripting (XSS).http://www.owasp.org, OWASP Top Ten Project, October 2010.

[Clim2011] Climm.org: Climm Instant Messaging Client. http://www.climm.org/ , Climm, February 2011.

[ICQB2007] BBC.org: AOL wins instant messaging case. http://news.bbc.co.uk/2/hi/technology/2591723.stm, BBC.org, December 2007.

[ICQC2011] ICQ.com: The ICQ Story. http://www.icq.com/info/story.html, ICQ.com, February 2011.

[Miran2011] Miranda.org: Addons. http://addons.miranda-im.org/, Miranda.org, February 2011.

[Owasp2009] Owasp.org: Category:OWASP Best Practices: Use of Web Application Firewalls, http://www.owasp.org/index.php/. Owasp.org, June 2009.

[Pidgi2011] Pigdin.im: About Pidgin, http://www.pidgin.im/about/. Pidgin.im, February 2011.

[Monit2011] Mircrosoft.com: Process Monitor v2.94, http://technet.microsoft.com/en-us/sysinternals/bb896645. Microsoft.com, January 2011.

[SVG2011] W3L.org: SCALABLE VECTOR GRAPHICS (SVG), http://www.w3.org/Graphics/SVG/. W3L.org, February 2011.

[Life2011] Squarefree.com: HTML life-editor, http://htmledit.squarefree.com/. February 2011.

[Wire2011] Wireshark.org: Wireshark Download, http://www.wireshark.org/download.html. Wireshark.org, February 2011.